CONCISE GUIDE
TO
TAROT

Text by
Gabriele Mandel

G000253414

Grange
BOOKS

© Copyright 1994 - I.G.L Lucchetti Service - Bergamo

Published By Grange Books
An Imprint of Grange Books PLC
The Grange, Grange Yard, London SE1 3AG
Published 1994

Printed in Italy by Litostampa I.G. - Gorle
ISBN 1 - 85627 - 577 - 2

THE TAROT

A BRIEF HISTORY OF THE TAROT

There are many Tarot packs around, but not all of them have developed from a single, ancient tradition. Some, indeed, belong to no tradition at all. They have simply been created by people ignorant of what the Tarot represents. We do not know exactly where or when the true Tarot pack first appeared. Different ideas have been put forward, but no one can be really sure and we must be content with a certain amount of conjecture and hypothesis. But having said that, a study of the Tarot can lead us on a fascinating and enjoyable adventure. And the cards themselves reveal some of the most extraordinary aspects of the mind of man.

Let us begin by describing the cards. The Tarot pack appears to be made up of two distinct groups. The first has 22 cards and is known as the Greater Arcana, once called the Trumps or Triumphs. These cards show symbolic figures: the Fool or Juggler, the Magician, the High Priestess, the Empress, the Emperor, the Pope, the Lover, the Chariot, Justice, Time, Fortune, Strength, the Hanged Man, Death, Temperance, the Devil, the Tower, the Star, the Moon, the Sun, Wisdom and the World.

The second group is composed of 56 numbered cards, called the Lesser Arcana, and is divided into four suits: swords, rods, cups and coins. Each suit has 14 cards numbered from 1 to 10, plus the Knave, Knight, King and Queen.

The cards with four suits may have developed from ancient oriental games and it is even possible that they were introduced to Europe by the "Saracens". But the 22 cards of the Tarot known as Trumps or Triumphs, although reminiscent of the avatars of Vishnu, appear to be rooted in the Renaissance. Indeed, the term "triumph", the old word for "trumps", takes us back to the

THE CHARIOT. Card made for Alesandro Sforza, Ferrara c. 1450/1460. Tarot pack from the Castello Ursino in Catania.

fifteenth century jousts and processions which took place in Italy.

The triumph developed from the ancient Roman tradition of making a great procession through the city to

*THE FOOL.
From the pack
made for
Charles VI,
Ferrara
1470/1480.
National
Library, Paris.*

honour victorious generals. In the middle ages the triumph took on a religious significance and could also be seen in the processions of knights before jousting contests. The classical taste for costumes, symbols and allegories also found expression here. In Florence, the triumph was mainly a musical spectacle with dancing. In the Duchy of Milan it was more of a ceremony involving triumphal chariots and processions of pages and damsels. Everywhere at Epiphany there were ceremonies involving the three Kings, King Herod, the

KING OF THE
EYES (VULCAN).
From the
Matteo Maria
Boiardo Tarot
pack, c. 1470.
Woodcut by
Pier Antonio
Viti of Urbino.

Star of Bethlehem and the Angel of the Annunciation. The processions which took place before jousting contests are evoked in present day fairground roundabouts, the wooden horses being reminiscent of the medieval knights.

*POMEGRANATE CARD.
From a game known as "Trap". First printed in Nuremberg c. 1400, subsequently revised by Wyonngottley in London c. 1790, then painted in water colours and tempera.*

Then there were public spectacles which derived from the literary Triumphs. They were based on the famous work by Petrach. This was composed of the Triumph of Chastity (card VI, Temperance), Fame (-card XXI), Time (card XI) and Eternity (card XIX).

THE SUN.
From the
Minchiate
Fiorentine,
Bologna 1775.
Woodcut.

The triumphal chariot also appears in card VII.

The Carnival King presided at the triumphal festivities, and he is represented in card I. The jousts and battles of real life were therefore reproduced in card games. While some of the cards were clearly rooted in real feelings and facts, such as the Wheel of Fortune, others are more obscure, such as the High Priestess or Female Pope. Nevertheless, this figure may have been connected with a real event as well since a female pope really did exist in the Visconti family. Also, in the thirteenth century, Wilhelmina of Bohemia founded a heretical sect, the Wilhelmites, who regarded her as the incarnation of the Holy Spirit sent to inaugurate the Age of the Spirit and fulfil the prophesy of Gioacchino da Fiore. Wilhelmina preached the coming of a female pope.

When Wilhelmina died in 1282, her work was continued by Andrea Saramita and Sister Manfreda Visconti of Pirovano. They were both burnt at the stake by the Inquisition in the autumn of 1300.

When the Tarot cards are placed next to one another they, too, form a procession, a Triumph, and describe in symbols some of the main aspects of fifteenth century society. Further evidence of the Renaissance origin of the Tarot is seen in the divinatory book published in Venice in 1526 by Jacomo Giunta, *The Triumph of Foutune,* by Sigismondo Fanti. This book is reminiscent of the I Ching in purpose, but it is richly illustrated with Tarot figures similar to those in the Mantegna Tarot. This pack is made up of 50 cards, which are not playing cards, and are divided into five groups of five cards each: 1) the Condition of Man (showing the letter E); 2) Apollo and the Muses (letter D); 3) Arts and Sciences (letter C); 4) Spirits and Virtues (letter B); 5) Planets and Spheres (letter A). In a later edition the first group shows the letter S. The pack was created by an anonymous Tarot Master from Ferrara in about 1465.

Other symbolic games are mentioned occasionally in the literature, which provide further evidence of the Tarot's connection with the Renaissance.

In Hind's *Catalogue of Early Italian Engravings* we find the following symbolic games listed in the Rosselli inventory: the "game of Petrarchan triumphs", a "game of apostles with Our Father, having seven wooden pieces", a "game of seven virtues, having 5 wooden pieces" and a "game of planets, having 4 pieces".

Of course, symbolic images were an important instrument of education and the church used them a long time before the invention of moveable type and the printing press. Just think of the *Biblia Pauperum,* which told the stories of the Old and New Testament in pictures for "poor" preachers who could not afford illuminated manuscripts.

Both the *Mantegna Tarot* and the *Biblia Pauperum* exploit the power and immediacy of symbols. The Tarot may symbolically reflect the Manichean dualistic heresy which became popular among the nobility in the fourteenth and fifteenth centuries. The Greater Arcana lends itself to this interpretation, although this dualistic significance was lost under the strict regime of the Inquisition and the Tarot survived only as a simple card game. This may explain why in Spain only the numbered cards appeared and not the Greater Arcana.

Yet it is also possible that the suits of the numbered cards have a symbolism all of their own. Some people see the suits as representing different classes of society: swords symbolize the nobility, the cups recall the chalice of the church and therefore represent the clergy, the coins represent the merchant class, and finally the rods are symbolic of the peasantry. Other people see the swords as representing justice, the rods as courage, the coins as charity and the cups as faith.

Different symbolic meanings were seen by such commentators as P. Ménestrier in 1704, Father Daniel in 1720 and Costant Leber in 1842, but apparently without much basis in reason or fact.

The Mantegna Tarot later inspired the use of cards as pictorial teaching aids. Here, the markings of the suits only took up a small amount of space. The rest of the card bore figures and captions having a purely didactic purpose. The inventor of these educational cards was Thomas Murner, the hard-headed adversary of Martin Luther. He printed his first "educational card game" in Cracow in 1507. A great many of Murner's packs were made, and even Stefano della Bella made engravings for four sets for the King of France in 1644.

THE DEVELOPMENT OF CARD GAMES

The first cards were probably made by hand and painted onto card, parchment or leather. They were the work of talented miniaturists and made, since they were so expensive, for the wealthy, noble classes. For this reason card playing remained within the confines of the private household, away from the eyes of the clergy or secular authorities. As a result we know very little about what kind of games were played. The best examples of hand made cards were around at the same time as the more

JUSTICE.
From the
Ligurian-
Piedmontese
Tarot. Mossi,
Turin, 1790.
Woodcut.

popular printed ones.

Among the miniaturists illustrating cards in the fifteenth century there were, in Ferrara, Alessandro Di Bartolomeo Quartesana, don Domenico Messere, Giovanni Di Lazzaro Cagnola and Petralcino from Florence. In 1415 Filippo Maria Visconti, the Duke of Milan, ordered a pack with a gold background. Between 1441 and 1447 the famous Visconti Sforza cards were made by Bonifacio Bembo, the only pack to come down to us today in more or less complete form.

But playing cards really became widespread when they began to be printed. The printed cards were either wood-

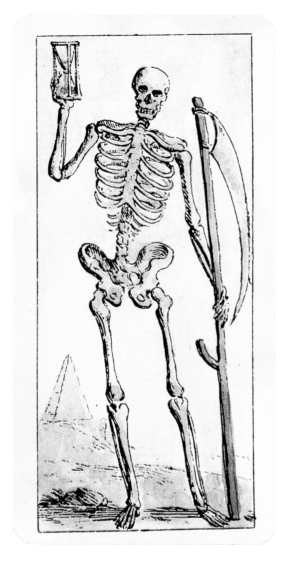

DEATH.
From the
Bolognese Tarot
made by
Giuseppe Maria
Mitelli, 1803.

cuts, which were popular in the Latin countries, or else made from copper engravings, which were more common in Germany.

At an early stage Italian cards were exported to Switzerland, South- East Germany, Austria, Bohemia,

Poland and Provence. When they were introduced into
Spain, the Italian cards (with the four suits of diamonds,
cups, rods and swords) did not have the Queens, the
eights, the nines or the tens. As a result there were only
40 cards.

Around 1450, new suits were introduced in Germany,
perhaps because the Germans wanted to monopolize the
market. The most widespread were hearts (Herzen), bells
(Schellen), leaves (Grum, or Laub) and acorns (Eicheln).
Instead of the Queen there was the Servant (Ober), and
the original servant became an *Unter*. The two (daus) sub-
stituted the Ace, and the pack had 48 cards. In Germany
the use of colour became an important means to the easy
and fast identification of the suits. The cards produced in
Germany were the work of highly talented artists. They
invented such fantastic and bizarre new suits, as unicorns,
deer, monkeys, rabbits, parrots, lions, swordsmen, books

and castles.

The craftsman playing-card maker who was active in the Upper Rhine around 1450 is the most important figure both in the history of cards in Germany as well as in the art of copper engraving. After him come Master ES, an artist of the most extraordinary talent and versatility, the Master of Bileam, Israel von Mechenen, Erhard Schoen, HS Berham, perhaps even Martin Schongauer, and, in the sixteenth century, Virgil Solis. A note by Ulma in 1474 tells us that Germany exported a great many cards to Italy, Sicily, Scandinavia, Poland, Austria and overseas.

Gradually, however, the cheaper woodcut cards made in France began to become more popular and widespread. They had new suits which probably derived from the German ones, but they were nevertheless more immediately accessible: hearts (from the German hearts), diamonds (perhaps from the bells or else the Swiss shields), spades (from the leaves), clubs (from the acorns or from the three German flowers). The French connect the introduction of the new suits to the action of the knight Etienne de Vignolles, who was one of Joan of Arc's followers.

Cards now began to acquire a definite form, even though the particular associations of each figure might vary. Around the end of the seventeenth century, for example, French cards evoked the following characters in the popular mind. The kings were identified with Alexander the Great, Ceasar, David and Charlemagne (a Greek, a Roman, a Hebrew and a European monarch). The queens became Rachel (beauty), Judith (faith), Pallas (wisdom) and Argina (nobility). The knights were La Hire, Ogier the Dane, Hector of France and Lancelot of the Round Table.

French supremacy in card making, which had been centred mainly in Lyon, began to decline in the eighteenth century, partly because of government fiscal policy. Only

*THE JUGGLER.
The first card of
the Italian
neo-classical
Tarot, made by
Ferdinando
Gumppenberg,
Milan c. 1810.*

Il Bagattelliere

Paris remained of any importance, but production never reached the heights of the previous centuries. Cards still continued to be made for the Spanish market, perhaps because they were similar in style to the early Tarot pack.

As Tarot production declined in importance some of the figures began to change form. This was actually due to the hurried copying of the cards by people who did not understand their significance. Time, for example, became the Hermit, the hour-glass being transformed into a lantern. Nevertheless, this same century saw a great revival of interest in the Tarot. Just as today people talk of flying saucers and other mysterious phenomena, in the eighteenth century they talked about the mysteries of Ancient

Egypt. They were fascinated by the temples, the unexplored tombs and a form of writing which had not yet been deciphered. It was on this basis that Antoine Court de Gebelin (1725 - 1784), a pastor of the Reformed Church, asserted that the Tarot was based on a mysterious Ancient Egyptian book which contained the secret of the meaning of human life. He compared the Tarot symbols to Egyptian hieroglyphics and came up with some startling and profound interpretations. The Egyptian connection, however, turned out to be lacking in any real basis in fact.

Court de Gebelin's interpretation of the Tarot had a great deal of influence among occultists and students of the esoteric sciences. One of his followers, a certain Etteila (his real name spelled backwards - Alliette), although lacking his teacher's erudition, produced some remarkable interpretations of the Tarot. He said that the Tarot had been created 3953 years before 1783 by seventeen Magi. The book they produced, called the Book of Thoth, contained all their knowledge. By changing the design of a few of the cards, Etteilla was able to produce an "Egyptian Tarot" for the specific purpose of divination. This interpretation proved to be very influential. And it was in this way that the systematic study of the Tarot as a means of prediction really got under way.

Another student of the Tarot, Alphonse Louis Constant, who lived in the nineteenth century and preferred to be known by the Hebrew version of his name - Eliphas Levi Zahed, connected the Tarot to the Cabbala, seeing in the Greater Arcana the sacred and occult alphabet created by Enoch. He equated the 22 cards with the 22 letters of the Hebrew alphabet, which were in turn linked to the Tree of Life.

The Cabbala is a symbolic system whose central idea is that the whole universe is the the expression of God the creator and that the world comes into being through miracle. Creation comes about by the naming of things, and therefore whoever possesses the Name, in writing and sound, is able to work miracles. Knowledge of God gives the ability to perform miracles. This condition is reached by means of the ten Sephiroths which emanate from God. Each of these ten Sephiroths is connected to three others by paths, and the whole of this arrangement is known as the Tree of Life. The 22 paths correspond to the 22 cards of the Greater Arcana of the Tarot.

The perfector of this idea was another Frenchman, Gerard Encausse (1865 - 1917), better known as Papus. He was the founder of the masonic order of the Martinists and a member of the cabbalistic Order of the

*THE KING OF
RODS.
Tarot from
Milan,
engraved by
Dalla Rocca,
printed by
F. Gumppenberg,
Milan, 1830.*

Rosicrucians.

In this way the Tarot acquired a definite origin and was considered to possess great occult powers. How much truth there is in all of this from a historical point of view is impossible to say. It is true that the Jews of Jerusalem consulted the oracle of Urin and Thumin and that this involved the use of symbolic figures (theraphim). And it is also true that the Tarot first began to appear in Italy at exactly the time when there was an increased interest in the Cabbala. But we canot say much more than this.

Another student of the occult, Dr Arthur Edward Waite (1857-1942) wrote: "The true Tarot is pure sumbolism. It speaks no other language and offers no other signs. Once

we have clarified the intrinsic significance of the symbols, we have a kind of alphabet capable of infinite combinations which are perfectly comprehensible. On the highest level, the Tarot provides the key to the Mysteries in a way which is neither obvious nor arbitrary. Nevertheless, there have been erroneous readings of the Tarot's symbolic meanings and books have been written which only represent falsehood."

However it may be, these writers aroused a great deal of interest in the Tarot and its divinatory powers. Today, new cards are still made which admit of novel and different interpretations.

*KING OF COINS.
From the same
Tarot pack as
the previous
card.
An unusual
version of the
Tarot having
historical
subjects.*

FORTUNE TELLING

PRATICAL EXAMPLES OF HOW TO READ THE TAROT

A brief interpretation of the meaning of the various figures making up the Tarot is given below each card.

There are various methods of reading and interpreting the Tarot. But in all of them the fortune teller should prepare himself by resting and fasting. The reading itself should be done in a quiet, darkened room. This is because the cards do not actually dictate what may lie in store in any objective way. Rather

Graz v. Nicolaiplatz.

they act as a catalyst, stimulating the divinatory powers of the fortune teller.

The person wishing to know his future shuffles the pack, cuts the cards and places them face down in front of the fortune teller. The cards are read individually, but their meaning is also determined by what cards have fallen before or come after.

The Ancient Method

Only the cards of the Greater Arcana are used. The fortune teller, with the shuffled and cut pack in front of him, turns the cards face up one by one and places them on the table in the following way:

```
              3         10
     6        1    4     9
              2         8
              5         7
```

Card number 1 shows the person's present situation; card 2 shows present influences; card 3 shows the person's destiny; card 4 describes the past; card 5 describes the recent past; card 6 shows the factors which will influence the future; card 7 represents the person whose fortune is being told; card 8 represents environmental factors; card 9 indicates the person's most intimate feelings and card 10 shows the final result of the consultation.

The Gypsy Method

The person wanting to know his future shuffles the cards of the Lesser Arcana, cuts the pack, removes the first twenty cards (which he must not see) and adds them to the Greater Arcana. The other cards are put aside. He now shuffles the cards and places them face down in seven groups of seven, starting from right to left. The fortune teller takes each group of cards and arranges them face up in parallel rows going from right to left. In this way he will obtain six rows of seven cards each. A card is chosen to represent the person whose fortune is being told (the Fool, Magician or Emperor for a man; the High Priestess or Empress for a woman). This card may be taken either from the cards laid out in rows or else from those which have been discarded. If the card is taken from those "in play", it is replaced by another taken from the discarded set. The reading is done from right to left, row after row, starting from the top. The first row represents past influences, the second represents present influences, the third repre-

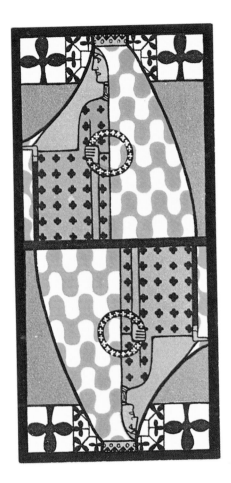

THE QUENN OF CLUBS. Tarot designed by the famous Viennese artist Ditha Moser. Piatnik & Sohne Edition, Vienna c. 1850.

sents eternal influences, the fourth represents the near future, the fifth shows future possibilities and the sixth indicates the final result and what the future has in store.

To Find a Job

Fan out the cards without looking at them and remove four cards. Then lay them out in a row going from left to right.

Let us suppose that the first card is number ten. This is the Wheel of Fortune and indicates the fulfil-

CARD *II*
OF THE VIENNESE
TAROT.
*Piatnik &
Sohne Edition,
Vienna 1860.
Coloured
lithograph.*

ment of any desire.

The second card might be number fifteen, the Devil. This indicates that there are obstacles to be overcome. The Devil represents the forces of Evil, the enemy of Good. This card shows that the two forces of Good and Evil will always be inextricably linked and that the one is unable to exist without the other.

The third card might be number twenty, Wisdom. This means that if difficulties arise in the search for a job, the person should not worry.

The fourth might be card number four, the Emperor.

This card indicates that the person is under the dominating influence of a strong character who is stifling his mental capacities. A powerful positive force will reach the dominating character and lead him to do good rather than evil actions.

If one wishes, at the end of the consultation, a card can be removed by chance which will either confirm or deny the result of the reading.

For Exams

Cut the pack and look at the bottom card of each half. These two cards give the meaning of the consultation.

Three cards are extracted: one for the day of the exam, one for the person consulting the cards and another to indicate the result. The number of the card is important here. If the last card has an odd number, there will be certain success.

THE POPE is a good card for the day of the exam since it indicates protection.

If WISDOM represents the person consulting the cards, this shows that his self-confidence will be rewarded by success.

STRENGTH means that despite the obstacles a firm resolve and clarity of thought will lead to certain success.

For the Future

Cut the pack and fan out the cards. Then remove ten cards from left to right and lay them out face down on the table to form a triangle. Place one row of four at the bottom, then one of three, then two cards and finally place one at the top. The reading begins.

Let us suppose that the first card is number 18, THE MOON. This indicates that there will be some disappointments and that people will oppose anything you

FORTUNE.
Tenth card of a
Bolognese Tarot
by Alessandro
Grandi,
Bologna 1862.
Woodcut.

try to achieve.

Then there might be card 13, DEATH. The appearance of this card should not cause excessive worry since it can be interpreted in a great variety of ways. Nevertheless, it does indicate the difficulties and problems which are inevitable in life.

The other cards might fall in this way:

Card number 4, THE EMPEROR. This means that anything you do or try to achieve depends on a person who lies outside your family and friends.

Card number 12, THE HANGED MAN. This shows

THE SUN.
Card XIX of a
Ligurian-
Piedmontese
Tarot by the
Avondo
Brothers,
Serravalle Sesia
1870. Metal en-
graving.

that you have become a slave who meekly perfoms all that is asked of him. This is due to weakness and a form of mental tiredness, but your opportunity for rebellion will come.

It is important to remember that all human beings tend to rebel against those who dominate them. And since rebellion is considered to have divine origins, we can regard man as a rebel against all that is unjust.

Number 14, TEMPERANCE. A re-awakening of vital energies will bring about a sudden change. This should be regarded as an auspicious sign and may indicate a journey and a marriage.

Number 2, the HIGH PRIESTESS. This means that

you will get what you want. A powerful protective force will guarantee the realization of your desires. Keeping your aims and plans secret is the best way to prevent other people from getting in the way of your ambitions.

Number 1, the JUGGLER. This card shows that you are searching for an explanation and have a deep desire to overcome your difficulties and avoid following a path that would lead nowhere.

Number 20, WISDOM. A firm decision will lead to financial gain and make the future easier. If you suffer from ill health you need not fear. You will slowly make a complete recovery.

Number 19, THE SUN. This indicates fulfilment, satisfaction and a happy marriage. It also indicates success in anything you do and may mean a chance to get a better paid job.

When the Sun appears among the other cards it also indicates a determined character with great powers of initiative.

Number 17, THE STARS. This card is auspicious and promises a future governed by intelligence and clarity.

This card represents the Spirit of Mind, the force which sustains and governs the whole of creation and whose Breath of Life produces the laws of motion and animates all living creatures.

These last two cards together show how a firm resolve can lead man to overcome the difficulties which are inherent in human life.

For Journeys

Shuffle the cards and cut the pack with the left hand. Hold the two halves suspended for a moment, then fan the cards and remove a number of cards to form two rows. The first should be made up of three cards and the other should have any number more than two.

Let us suppose that the cards fall in this way:

The first is number 7, THE CHARIOT. This indicates difficulties have been overcome but that a few small problems will delay the departure. Nevertheless, it is a good card and indicates success.

Number 16, THE TOWER. Indecision causes important plans to fail. But this need not be totally bad

*KING OF CLUBS.
Piatnik &
Sohne Edition,
Budapest-
Vienna c. 1870.*

since there is a glimmer of hope that something positive and definite will turn up.

Number 6, THE LOVERS. It might appear to be the right moment for the realization of a number of things, but an unexpected meeting will lead to problems.

Number ten, STRENGTH. It is vital not to lose heart and work slowly and carefully towards the real-

*KING OF COINS.
Ligurian-
Piedmontese
Tarot by Pietro
Oletti, Turin
1875.*

RE DI DANARI

ization of your objectives. Any temptation to give way to impulsiveness must be held in check.

Number 21, THE WORLD. When all seems lost there will be a sudden change that will lead to success.

For a Marriage

Proceed in the same way as for the other readings, then choose five cards and lay them out on the table in the form of a cross.

Let us consider the following possibility:

The first card at the top might be number 2, THE

EIGHT OF HEARTS. Tyrol playing cards by Andreas Hofer, Hayman Edition, Innsbruck c. 1878.

HIGH PRIESTESS. This is an auspicious card for marriage and family life in general. It also indicates the overcoming of difficulties.

The central card might be number 7, THE CHARIOT. This is a positive card for men and women and indicates success and the strength to overcome the inevitable difficulties of life.

Even if the other cards turn out to be negative, this need not matter. It is the first two that really count in this reading and together provide a sound basis for the creation of harmony and cooperation.

For a Lawsuit

Before beginning the reading it is necessary to concentrate the mind on the idea of a successful out-

THE SUN.
Card 36 of a
modern
Minchiata
Fiorentina,
produced by
Vito Arienti.
Woodcut by
Costante
Costantini,
Lissone 1981.

come. Fan the pack, remove three cards and arrange them in a triangle. Place another card in the middle. This serves as a witness or key card.

Let us suppose that the first card is number 4, THE EMPEROR. This is a good card. It indicates clarity and intelligence and is therefore a sign of success.

Then there might be number 16, THE TOWER. An unexpected and unpleasant event will cause a temporary setback, but eventually things will be put right.

Then there might be number 21, THE WORLD. This indicates a definitive change for the better. Such qualities as courage and determination combined with a pleasant cheerfulness help keep self-doubt at bay.

The central card, the witness, is the most important. Let us suppose that it is number 10, THE WHEEL OF FORTUNE. This card indicates unexpected events and the overcoming of difficulties. It particularly indicates good health, which is the preserver of existence and establishes an ordered and well-balanced life.

All things considered, it is a very favourable card signifying love and riches.

For the Health of a Member of the Family

Proceed in the same way as for the other readings. Remove three cards and lay them out vertically. Let us suppose that the first one is number 16, THE TOWER. It is not a bad card because it indicates wisdom and common-sense, as well as an understanding of what is right and reasonable and breadth of vision. Even if you are in ill health and feel down, the card will give you faith in the support of your family.

The second might be number 9, THE HERMIT. This card represents wisdom and caution. It means that the family member's health depends on the choice of an honest and reliable doctor who is able to lead the ill person back towards health.

There are certain immutable natural laws which must on no account ever be forgotten. Otherwise man will suffer, his body will become unbalanced and he will inevitably need medical help.

The third card might be number 10, FORTUNE. This is quite a good card and indicates the overcoming of difficulties. There is no reason to fear for the health of the ill person, who will respond favourably to treatment, although there are bound to be ups and downs.

If you wish to have a confirmation of what the cards have revealed, you can choose two cards as witnesses. Place these next to each other to the right of the verticle row.

Let us suppose that one of them is number 8, JUS-TICE. This card represents moral integrity, faith and

SOLLEONE TAROT

settantotto nuove carte create
da ELISABETTA CASSARI
con la provocazione stimolante
di Vito Arienti

EDIZIONI DEL SOLLEONE

Copyright © by Vito Arienti Editore
Dicembre 1981
I 20035 Lissone (Mi) Italia

family affection. All these positive things keep anxiety at bay and provide relief.

The other card might be number 18, THE MOON.

11 - LA PAPESSA

THE HIGH PRIESTESS

THE HIGH PRIESTESS. CARD XI of the modern Tarot "Homage to Erté" by A. Folchi. Printed by vito Arienti, Lissone 1985.

This is a stange card. Despite its suggestion of deception, danger and falsehood, it also offers protection. It shines at night and therefore has a benign influence. It leads man to act in harmony with the world, with the Universal Power, with the Supreme Essence, with every individual thing, high or low, near or far, visible or invisible. It brings understanding in love and leads the individual to the discovery of his innermost self. This opens the way to the Heavenly kingdom, or rather the Mystic Kingdom of God, the Supreme.

In this way you can obtain a confirmation of the reading which should remove any possible doubt.

THE MEANING OF THE CARDS

In giving the sequence and symbolic meaning of the Tarot cards, I should make clear that other sequences of the Greater Arcana exist, although they seem to be less historically sound. As for the symbolic meaning of the various cards, a great variety of different interpretations is possible. My comments here are necessarily brief for reasons of space. The correspondence to astrological signs and to the numbers and letters of the Hebrew alphabet follow the version given by Eliphas Levi and Papus. Other writers differ in their treatment.

The "Greater Arcana" reproduced here is the *Visconti-Sforza Tarot* made by Bonifacio Bembo and Antonio Cicognara. The "Lesser Arcana" is the work of Giuseppe Maria Mitelli.

The Fool

Either zero or no number. Atonement and suffering. A negative symbol indicating a passive, submissive attitude, impulsiveness, foolishness and a carefree approach to life. This card became the joker in modern playing cards. Astrological symbol: Scorpio. Number: 300. Hebrew letter: Shin. Together with the Juggler or Magician, its oposite card, it represents the subject of the consultation.

I - The Juggler
(Magician or Carnival King).

Willpower. An active, positive symbol indicating initiative, self-confidence, wisdom, reason, creativity and the ability to achieve desired objectives. Astrological symbol: Sun. Number: 1. Hebrew letter: Aleph. Its opposite card is the Fool (see above).

II - The High Priestess

Science. This card indicates intuition, the power to know the future, the penetration of mysteries, knowledge, arcane wisdom and practical ability. Astrological symbol: Moon. Number: 2. Hebrew letter: Bet. Together with the World, its opposite, it allows the perception of the unknown. In the fifteenth century it occupied position IV.

III - The Empress

Action. This card indicates observation, understanding, conception, study, wisdom, female progress, fertility and material wealth. Astrological symbol: Earth. Number: 3. Hebrew letter: Gimel. Together with Wisdom, its opposite, it symbolizes the assimilation of the external world. In the fifteenth century it occupied position XV.

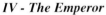

IV - The Emperor

Achievement. This card indicates earthly powers, authority, the ability to command and act independently, inner light, the word become flesh, energy, analytical skills and virtue. Astrological symbol: Jupiter. Number: 4. Hebrew letter: Daleth. Together with the Sun, its opposite, it means spiritual knowledge. In the fifteenth century it occupied position III.

V - The Pope

Inspiration. This card represents ritual, tradition, the inability to adapt, abstract ideas, metaphysics, religion, spirituality, forgiveness, transcendental knowledge and submission to morality. Astrological symbol: Mercury. Number: 5. Hebrew letter: Heh. Together with the Moon, its opposite, it represents the production of a synthesis.

VI - Love
(The Lover)

Trial. The card represents love, beauty, freedom, choice and doubt. It indicates a restless struggle with the difficulties of life and love, the emotions, an important relationship and rivalry. Astrological symbol: Virgo. Number: 6. Hebrew letter: Vau. Together with the Stars, its opposite card, it represents determination in action. In the fifteenth century it occupied position VIII.

VII - The Chariot

Victory. This card indicates the overcoming of difficulties, balance, caution, talent, success, progress, harmony, the need to plan. Astrological symbol: Sagittarius. Number: 7. Hebrew letter: Zain. Together with the Tower, its opposite, it represents the mind in its struggle to understand matter.

VIII - Justice

Balance. This card indicates reasonableness, stability, logic, calm and common sense. Astrological symbol: Libra. Number: 8. Hebrew letter: Chet. Together with the Devil it represents the organization and control of force. In the fifteenth century it occupied position XX.

IX - Time
(the Hunchback of the Hermit)

Caution. This card indicates common sense, care, isolation, meanness, the painstaking and methodical search for knowledge and a lack of drive. Astrological symbol: Neptune. Number: 9. Hebrew letter: Teth. Together with Temperance it indicates the reation of the individual with the environment. In the fifteenth century it occupied position XI.

X - The Wheel
*(Fortune of the Wheel
of Fortune)*

Fortune. This card indicates ambition, fate, the solution of problems, invention, discovery, the seeds of life, change and evolution. Astrological symbol: Capricorn. Number 10. Hebrew letter: Iod. Together with Death it indicates the intervention of the fates.

XI - Strength

Strength. This card indicates consiousness, conquest, the putting into practice of ideas, the domination of matter, energy, action, virility and resistance. Astrological symbol: Leo. Number: 20. Hebrew letter: Kaph. Together with the Hanged Man this card indicates realization of an aim or objective. In the fifteenth century it occupied position IX.

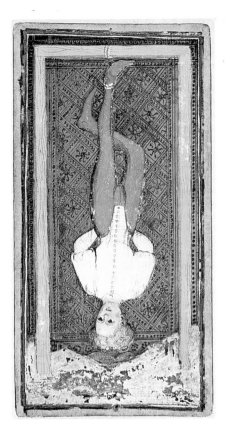

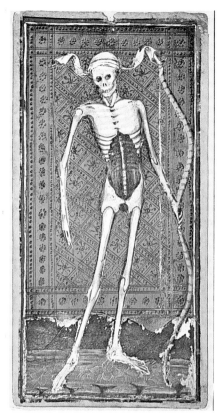

XII - The Traitor
(the Hanged Man)

Sacrifice. This card indicates life in the balance, impotence, unreality, dream, martyrdom for others' ignorance, a break and repentance. Astrological symbol: Uranus. Number: 30. Hebrew letter: Lamed. Makes a pair with Strength (see above).

XIII - Death

Death. This card indicates fatality, disappointment, sacrifice, loss, failure, illness, change and renewal. Astrological symbol: Saturn. Number: 40. Hebrew letter: Men. Makes a pair with the Wheel (see above).

XIV - Temperance

Initiative. This card indicates moderation, patience, adaptation, participation, togetherness, openness, extravagance, medical ability and excessive caution. Astrological symbol: Aquarius. Number: 50. Hebrew letter: Nun. Makes a pair with Time (see above). In the fifteenth century it occupied position VI.

XV - The Devil

Fatality. This card indicates wildness, a fall, disorder, instinct, rage, burning passion, lack of principles and a loathing of advice from others. Astrological symbol: Mars. Number: 60. Hebrew letter: Samech. Makes a pair with Justice (see above). In the fifteenth century it occupied position XIV.

XVI - The Tower
(the House of God,
the House of the Devil
or the House of Pluto)

Ruin. This card indicates a sudden change, a break, adversity, a catastrophe, infatuation or a change of faith. Astrological symbol: Aries. Number: 70. Hebrew letter: Ain. Makes a pair with the Chariot (see above). In the fifteenth century it occupied position XV.

XVII - The Star
(The Heavenly Body, the Stars)

Hope. This card indicates a benign influence, light, predestination, a complete trust in the future and the idea of immortality, idealism and a taste for beauty. Astrological symbol: Venus. Number: 80. Hebrew letter: Peh. Makes a pair with Love (see above). In the fifteenth century it occupied position XVI.

XVIII - The Moon

Deceit. This card indicates trickery, dishonesty, illusion, superstition, materialism, mistakes, prejudice, capriciousness and lies. Astrological symbol: Cancer. Number: 90. Hebrew letter: Tzadd. Makes a pair with the Pope (see above). In the fifteenth century it occupied position XVII.

XIX - The Sun

Happiness. This card indicates satisfaction, achievement, altruism, eternal and universal light, growth, flashes of insight, serenity, poetry and the fine arts. Astrological symbol: Gemini. Number: 100. Hebrew letter: Qoph. Makes a pair with the Emperor (see above). In the fifteenth century it occupied position XVIII.

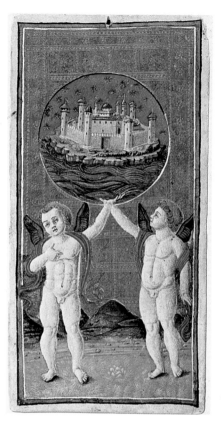

XX - The Angel
(Wisdom)

Renewal. This card indicates atonement, inspiration, enthusiasm, repentance, the need to behave honestly. Astrological symbol: Pisces. Number: 20. Hebrew letter: Resh. Makes a pair with the Empress (see above). In the fifteenth century it occupied position XIX.

XXI - The World

Reward. This card indicates achievement, completeness, success, ecstasy, triumph, success at work and absolute knowledge. Astrological symbol. Taurus. Number: 400. Hebrew letter: Tau. Makes a pair with the High Priestess (see above).

SWORDS. *King:* a decisive, active and important person. *Queen:* a wise and sharp-witted person. *Knight:* courage, skill, heroism. *Knave:* care, help and discretion. *Ten:* benefit, profit. *Nine:* depression, worry and argument. *Eight:* crisis, calamity. *Seven:* positive plans, hope. *Six:* invitation, travel. *Five:* uncertainty, loss and conflict. *Four:* rest, solitude and relaxation. *Three:* pain, disappointment and struggle. *Two:* falseness, deceit and hostility. *Ace:* strength, vigour, triumph and power.

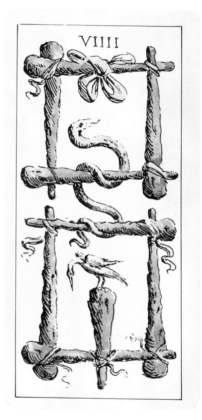

RODS. *King:* defender, loyal friend, help. *Queen:* sincere affection and honesty. *Knight:* travel, escape or a change of scene. *Knave:* faithfulness, messenger, good news. *Ten:* exhaustion, problems and selfishness. *Nine:* difficulties, enemies and deceit. *Eight:* activity, progress, quick promotion. *Seven:* success, financial gain and victory. *Six:* triumph, conquest, good news. *Five:* struggle, fatigue, dissatisfaction. *Four:* harmony, peace and falling in love. *Three:* sharpness, enterprise, commercial success. *Two:* support, achievement. *Ace:* invention, production, creativity, luck, inheritance, birth, adventure.

CUPS. *King:* responsibility, creation, self-employment. *Queen:* devoted mother, an intelligent and sensitive woman. *Knight:* invitation, opportunity, advancement. *Knave:* reflective person, loyal, helpful. *Ten:* home, happiness, family harmony. *Nine:* success, well-being, health, victory. *Eight:* disappointment, a break, harmful shyness. *Seven:* Utopian dreams, wishful thinking, dreams, silliness. *Six:* memories, tradition, nostalgia, ambition. *Five:* loss, regret, marriage without love. *Four:* dislike, disgust, bitter experience. *Three:* solution to problems, relief, recovery from sickness, agreement. *Two:* love, friendship, passion, marriage, union. *Ace:* Abundance, wealth, joy, future happiness.

COINS. *King:* expert manager, excellent businessman, a skilful investor. *Queen:* prosperity, well-being, luxury, material satisfaction, nobility. *Knight:* a good organizer, trustful, efficient, sure. *Knave:* hard work, study, commitment, work, respect for values. *Ten:* prosperity, wealth, family security, inheritance. *Nine:* danger, robbery, loss of goods or inheritance. *Eight:* skilful crafstmanship, openness, constancy and modesty. *Seven:* hard work, development, treasure, determination at work. *Six:* generosity, philanthropy, gifts, rewards. *Five:* financial difficulties, loss of work, mistakes, lovers. *Four:* meanness, usury, inability. *Three:* commercial or artistic skill, dignity, success. *Two:* difficulties, unexpected troubles, worry. *Ace:* perfection, achievement, happiness, well-being, riches, prosperity.

You can play many kinds of games with the Tarot pack. All you have to remember is that the Greater Arcana or Trumps beat all Trumps lower than them, the highest card being number 21 and the lowest being zero, the Fool. The Trumps always beat the Lesser Arcana or suits. Usually, however, the Angel (number 20) beats the World (number 21), and thus becomes the highest card.

The numbered cards form an obvious scale of values, but there are two exceptions. The Ace of Cups and the Ace of Coins beat cards of their respective suits from two to ten. In counting the points won, the Trumps and Kings count five points each (however, the Fool in the Game of Sixteen and the Game of Thirty One only counts one point), Queens four points, Knights three, Knaves two and Aces one.

The Game of Sixteen

In this game you need sixteen points to win. The first player to do so leaves the game. Deal four cards to each player. The player to the right of the dealer leads. The other players must follow suit, Trumps with Trumps, coins with coins, and so on.

Only if a player lacks the required suit can he play a Trump or other suit of his choice. In the latter case, however, no matter how high the card is, he cannot win the round. The round is won by the player who puts down the highest card of the required suit, plays a Trump or plays the highest Trump card. At the end of the round, deal another four cards and continue the game.

The Game of Thirty One

This game is exactly the same as the previous one except that you deal eight cards and you need thirty one points to win.

The Game of Baronets

This is a game for two players. The dealer places a row of ten cards face down in front of his opponent. The last card of the row is placed face up. Then he places a similar row in front of himself, then another in front of his opponent, then another in front of himself, always leaving the last card face up, until there are four rows before the two players. This last row will only have nine cards. The player who has not dealt leads the game. He plays one of his face up cards, and the other player follows, similarly playing one of his face up cards. After this the players turn up one of their face down cards. The winner of the round then leads with another face up card and the game continues as before until one of the players has gained 46 points. The pictured cards only count if they are accompanied by a discarded card of the same suit.

Tarot for Three, "May I?" or Terziglio

The dealer gives 25 cards to each of the other two players, takes 28 for himself and discards three face down on the table saying, "I've discarded". The next player asks "May I?" and if the other two players reply, "Go", he discards three cards from his own hand and asks the other two players for the two cards he wants. As they give him the cards, the two players pick up the same number of cards

from the ones the first player has discarded. After this the game begins, and the one who asked "May I?" plays alone against the other two, who, although keeping their cards hidden from one another, add their points together. 46 points are needed to win.

However, if before the game begins the next player answers "Two" to the request "May I?", and the other players say "Go", only the player who said "Two" may discard. But he must discard and pick up only two cards. He then plays alone against the other two, as in the previous case. If the third player replies "I go for one" instead of "Go", and the others accept, then only he discards and plays alone against the others. If a player asks to "Pick up", he does not discard at all and he plays against the other two. In other words, the one who asks to discard the least number of cards plays against the other two. Should there be a disagreement, the leading player - the one to the right or to the left of the dealer, as agreed before the game - has the right to decide.

To play "May I?" with four players

(Quartiglio) deal nineteen cards. The dealer discards two.

To play "May I?" with five people (Quintilio), deal fifteen cards. The dealer discards three.

To play "May I?" with six people (Sestilio), deal thirteen cards. There will be no cards to discard.

To play "May I?" with seven people (Settilio), deal eleven cards. The dealer will only have one card to discard.

The winner of these games is the one who has more points than all the other players put together.

Other games that can be played with the Tarot pack are: the Game of 22 Cards played by two people, the Game of the Dead Man, the Game of the Doctor, the Game of the Least, the Game of Calling King, the Game of All Cards, the Game of the Meek, the Game of Three, the Game of "Bagattultimo", and the Game of Advice.

Solitaire

Solitaire is a card game played individually having no other result than that of success or failure. Many people believe that it is possible to read a horoscope in the result of a game of solitaire. Below are a few examples of solitaire games or "readings" created by some well-known ladies in the history of the Tarot. They are really methods of interpreting the Tarot cards for individuals. These fashionable ladies created them for the visitors to their salons. Later they began to be used by fortune tellers genrally.

Lola Montes's Method

Lola took nine cards from the Greater Arcana and arranged them carefully in the following way: THE JUGGLER at the top, THE HERMIT and THE POPE below, THE HIGH PRIESTESS to the right, THE EMPRESS AND EMPEROR below, JUSTICE to the left, and THE CHARIOT and THE LOVERS below.

The beautiful Lola Montez then concentrated on what she wanted to know and began the reading from the first to the ninth card, going from left to right. If there was not a satisfying result, she added four cards taken at random from the pack, placing them at the four corners. If she found the card which represented her among these four cards, then the reading could be considered to have worked well and in all probability her wishes would be realized.

As a fixed card she usually chose THE SUN, the Highest Heavenly Body, which symbolizes clarity of mind and splendour. As a witness, she put next to this a special ancient card which represented the god Momus, once considered the spirit of joy. When this card falls, it signifies great joy and well-being.

The Magic Circle

Diane Cleopatre de Merode began to become interested in magic and card reading when she was still very young. She took the name of Cleo and began wearing oriental clothes and exotic jewellery. The Marahaja of Kapurthala, who was one of her admirers, gave her a ring set with a diamond the size of a hazel nut.

Cleo de Merode was among the esoteric circle created by Papus, and here she learned a lot about the rites of Egyptian magic.

She was expert at reading the Tarot and only used the Greater Arcana. She created a method of reading known as the "Magic Circle".

She took nine cards at random from the pack and arranged them in a circle. In the middle she placed two cards which she had had especially designed for the purpose. One showed the double triangle of Solomon's Seal. In the middle there was an eagle, below which were two spirals. The descending spiral represented the creation of matter by spirit, and the ascending spiral symbolized man's progress towards perfection.

The other card showed the famous Witch of Endor, whom Saul had consulted before the battle of Gelboè, and at the bottom there was the Sacred Fire. Because of its pureness, fire was considered the noblest of the four elements. It was also the one which came closest to the divine, in the sense that it was considered to be the image of the Light of Day.

The first card represented Cleo, the reader, while the second served as a guide. With this method of reading she obtained great success and practised the method for her friends. The cards were always different and the reading could be repeated several times until the desired result was achieved. It was not a difficult method, but it required patience and concentration. Her special cards were a vital aid to her psychic powers and the creation of the correct magical atmosphere to ensure the reading's success.